THEY DIED TOO YOUNG

JIM MORRISON

BY

Jon E. Lewis

This edition first published by Parragon Books Ltd in 1995

Produced by
Magpie Books Ltd, London

Unit 13–17, Avonbridge Trading Estate
Atlantic Road
Avonmouth
Bristol BS11 9QD

Illustrations courtesy of: Rex Features.

ISBN 0 75250 705 2

A copy of the British Library Cataloguing in Publication Data is available from the British Library.

Typeset by Hewer Text Composition Services, Edinburgh
Printed in Singapore by Printlink International Co.

A Life Ends, A Life Begins

In the summer of 1949 Steve and Clara Morrison were taking the kids on holiday. As their Oldsmobile cruised the desert highway outside Albuquerque, and a dawn storm crackled in the far peaks, they passed an upturned truck. Some injured Pueblo Indians were lying on the road. Steve stopped the car and got out and asked the traffic cop if there was anything he could do to help. Returning to the car, Steve found his

5-year-old son Jimmy staring through the window and sobbing 'I want to help' and 'They're dying!', over and over. Jimmy was inconsolable. Desperate, Steve said, 'It didn't really happen, Jimmy. It was just a dream. Just a dream.'

When the Morrisons' car pulled away from the accident, Jimmy, still crying, looked out through the rear window. As he did so, an old Indian medicine man who was lying on the side of the road, his eyes on Jimmy, smiled and died.

Years later, when he had become a rock star, Jimmy would say that this 'was the most important moment in my life', for Jimmy believed that as the shaman died his soul entered Jimmy's body. Henceforth Jim Morrison was destined to become a seeker of the truths that lie on the other side of reality, in the spirit world, in the unknown. The rest – the rebelliousness, the looks of a Greek god, the genius, the death wish, the wild living – came from his family and his times.

The result was always going to be explosive. But for a brief period, 1965 to 1971, three musicians managed to harness the power of Jim Morrison, dark and shooting star, to form the greatest – and the most controversial – American rock 'n' roll group of all time: The Doors.

James Douglas Morrison was a war baby. He was born on 8 December, 1943, in Melbourne, Florida, near where his navy father was training to fly Hellcats against the Japanese in the Pacific. The only son of a Florida laundry owner, Steve had met Jim's mother, the good-looking Clara Clarke, at a dance in December 1941, just after the bombing of Pearl Harbor. As was the fashion in war time, the couple married quickly, in April 1942.

Steve returned from the war a hero, an officer and a gentleman, and decided to make a career in the navy. The Morrisons – the family soon expanded to include a daughter, Anne, and another son, Andy – became comfortably off as the 1940s rolled into Eisenhower's silver-lined 1950s. And Jim, handsome if somewhat chubby, enjoyed a typical American boyhood, swimming – he was a superb swimmer – reading *Mad* magazines, goofing off, bulling his younger brother, peeking at girls undressing into their bathing suits. He was always ferociously intelligent (his IQ was 149) and he coasted through school without even having to try. He seemed, by his teens, to have read everything. His favorite authors were the new Beat writers like Jack Kerouac, and the German philosopher of despair, Friedrich Nietzsche.

But most of all he admired the French Symbolist poet Arthur Rimbaud, the archetypal Romantic literary hero, dead at 19 after turning to slave-running in the heart of dark Africa. 'A poet', said Rimbaud, 'makes himself a visionary through a long, boundless, and systematized disorganization of all the senses.' It was a belief that Jim would come, in time, to take as his own.

Soon Jim was not just reading others but writing himself, filling up notebooks with stories, thoughts and, especially, poems. Some of these would surface years later as the lyrics for Doors' songs, including 'Horse Latitudes' and 'Peace Frog'. A number were about death and water.

If part of Jim's youth was gilded, part was not. As a navy family, the Morrisons were constantly on the move, uprooted almost as soon as they had moved into a new house in a new state – anywhere the navy said. To get attention in a new school Jim, painfully shy, would tell tall tales (he once claimed, convincingly, to his class that he had to have a brain tumor removed), and be deliberately provocative to see what would earn a response.

At home, Jim's life was far from idyllic. His mother was domineering, his father an increasingly remote figure, rarely seen by the family as he climbed higher and higher up the naval ladder. Later Jim would become so estranged from his parents that he never wrote, spoke to or saw them. In the 'bio sketch' which accompanied the Doors' first album he would even claim they were dead.

Throughout his senior year of high school, the George Washington in Alexandria, Virginia, Jim's mother pressured him into going to college. Since Jim showed no interest, she enrolled him in the autumn of 1961 at the establishment of her choice, St Petersburg Junior College, where he could board with Steve's parents in nearby Clearwater, Florida.

The conservative home town of his grandparents was misnamed; backwater, maybe. To kill the smallville boredom Jim started drinking, and hanging out at the one bohemian place in town, the Renaissance Gallery. Other devices were less harmful. He would help buddies with their college work – Jim always went out of his way for his friends – like the time he wrote one of them an expert 30-page essay on the Elizabethan courtier Lord Essex, complete with references and footnotes, off the top of his head.

He also fell in love.

It happened at a party, when Jim was doing a daredevil walk along the balcony wall of a second level apartment. (Throughout his life, Jim would display a tendency for dangerous stunts on high buildings.) When Jim started to fall, the girl standing closest pulled him in.

Mary Frances Werbelow was sweet sixteen, two years younger than Jim, and had been a runner up in that summer's local Sun N Fun Beauty Contest. She took Jim walking barefoot in the morning dew, Jim showed her his poetry journals and got her to wear sunglasses, outraging local mores.

A year later Jim moved to Tallahassee to enrol at Florida State University, hitching over 200 miles to Clearwater at weekends to see Mary. It was at FSU that Jim, previously claiming to 'hate' rock 'n' roll, became addicted to Elvis, playing Presley records all day, all night. When Jim's roommates in FSU campus accomodation could finally stand no more of the King, and the reverence that Jim insisted on (including silence whenever an Elvis record came on the radio), they told him to 'straighten up'. Jim smiled his smile and moved out that night, living thereafter in a caravan behind a girls' school and at Room 206 of the downtown Cherokee Hotel, sometime hooker's haunt. Jim loved it.

Along with his Elvis obsession, Jim was beginning to develop a serious interest in film. Soon, he was itching to get out of FSU and enrol at film school in Los Angeles. His parents forbade it. So he laboured on at FSU until finally presenting his parents with a *fait accompli*: he had enrolled at UCLA Film School, starting classes in January 1964.

Jim Morrison

Jim moved to Los Angeles in 1964

Doors Close, Doors Open

A gifted student, Jim was entered on an accelerated two-year programme at UCLA film school, then enjoying an international reputation. Josef von Sternberg, amongst other industry luminaries, was on the staff, and the students included the likes of the young Francis Ford Coppola.

In May 1965, Jim's student film was shown at the UCLA film theatre. His piece was an abstract medley of images, 'questioning', Jim said, 'the film process itself'. A film about film. As a clip of Jim smoking grass was followed by a clip of a girl in suspenders atop a television showing marching Nazis, a chorus of derision started up. There were catcalls and boos. Never one to take criticism lightly, Jim got out of his seat, where he had been hiding with his jacket over his head, and walked out. He paused only to say, 'I quit'. Since the semester had only a few weeks to run he was given his diploma anyway.

Film school wasn't the only thing Jim quit in the summer of 1965. Mary Werbelow had moved to LA to join Jim, but it was not working out. They argued when Mary said she might get a job as a go-go dancer (Jim had a conservative streak, which occasionally surfaced, to everyone's surprise), they argued about the amount of LSD tablets Jim was popping, they argued about Jim seeing other girls. And then it was over.

Jim had already put his family behind him. He had visited his parents at Christmas, the last time he would ever see them.

If some doors were closing, others were opening. Walking across campus in June, Jim bumped into Ray Manczarek, a blond haired, bespectacled intellectual, four years older than Jim, who was regarded as one of the top students in the cinematography department. Ray needed someone to fill a temporary spot in his band, Rick and the Ravens, who were scheduled to play support to Sonny and Cher at a high school graduation, but were stuck with a union obligation for a sixth member. Ray asked Jim if he would play a gig with the band. Jim explained, in his voice so soft you had to strain to catch it, that he couldn't play an instrument. No problem, said Ray, they would just get him to stand there with an electric guitar, but not plug it into the amps.

It was Jim's first paying gig, and he did not sing or play a note. He would always maintain that it was the easiest money he ever earned.

With the finish of school Jim moved to Venice, LA's alternative quarter. The hippie era had arrived. LSD was sold over the counter, the Beach Boys were on car radio, and all the girls were Californian, with flowers in their hair.

The assault on the senses sent Jim into a frenzy of creation, the like of which he would never experience again. He seldom ate, slept only for a few hours a night – usually at the canalside shack of UCLA friend, Denis Jakob, – but always writing, writing, writing. The songs just poured out. 'It was like taking notes', he said, 'at a fantastic rock concert going on inside my head.'

A beautiful black girl walking along the beach front ('Do you hope to pluck this dusky jewel') prompted 'Hello, I Love You', a future number 1 single, to emerge almost fully formed. Olivia's, a small cheap restaurant near the Venice arcade, occasioned 'Soul Kitchen'. 'Moonlight Drive' and 'Celebration of the Lizard' were also written at this time. There were sheets more. And all bore what would become the Morrison hallmark: startling visual imagery, and an obsession with darkness, water and death. Even a love song like 'Moonlight Drive' ended with 'Baby gonna drown tonight/Go down, down, down . . .'

The songs were ready. And he felt a compulsion to sing them himself; the lyrics were too precious, too personal to give to someone else. All he had to do now was find a band.

Opportunity knocked in August of that year, when he once again bumped into Ray Manczarek, this time on Venice beach. Jim told Ray about his songs, and Ray later recalled asking Jim to sing one for him. 'He sat down on the beach and said, 'Okay, here's one I got. It's called "Moonlight Drive'."

'When I heard the first lines, "Let's swim to the tide/Let's swim to the moon . . .", I said, "Wow, that's it, man. Those are the greatest f—— lyrics I've ever heard. Let's form a band and make a million".'

This was just the idea Jim had in mind himself. He even had a name for the band: The Doors. He had taken it from the title of Aldous Huxley's drug tome

The Doors of Perception. Huxley in turn had taken it from a phrase by the poet William Blake: 'If the doors of perception were cleansed everything would appear to man as it is, infinite.'

Jim said he wanted the band to be the doors between the known and the unknown.

The heart of the hippie scene was in California

The Doors

Breaking On Through

Soon after the meeting on Venice beach, Ray invited Jim to move into the Ocean Park garage apartment he shared with his Japanese-American girlfriend, Dorothy Fujikawa. There Jim slept on the couch and they worked on the songs all day while Dorothy was at work.

At Ray and Dorothy's Jim popped peyote and LSD pills by the dozen to 'expand' his head and raise his consciousness, and wrote lyrics that seemed like an acid trip in themselves . . . weird scenes inside the gold mine . . . break on through to the other side . . . the face in the mirror won't stop.

His singing voice was, he and Ray agreed, quiet and weak but would get stronger with practice. In the meantime, he chant-sung the lyrics and Ray, a classically trained pianist with a liking for the blues, began working up an accompanying sound on his keyboards.

After two weeks Ray took Jim to his parents' house at Manhattan Beach where Rick and the Ravens rehearsed. Jim's psychedelic lyrics didn't do much for Ray's brothers, Jim and Rick

Manczarek, but they agreed to join the band. The line up, though, badly needed a drummer – and then Ray remembered that a guy in his Transcendental Meditation class was a drummer.

Educated at University High School in LA, the middle-class son of an architect, John Densmore had been playing drums since the age of 12. He was a jazz freak, much influenced by the loose, stream of consciousness style of John Coltrane and Miles Davis. He had recently dropped out of San Fernando Valley State and decided to take a chance at being a musician.

So, one Saturday morning John turned up at Ray's parents' garage, was introduced to Ray's brothers and a quiet guy in T-shirt, jeans and bare feet in the corner, 'Jim, our singer'. Ray also showed John, in the manner of a proud uncle, some of Jim's lyrics to a song called 'Break on Through'. John was hooked – even more so when Morrison sang. If his singing was tentative, with Morrison clutching the lyric sheets for security (though he knew all the words), he had charisma. 'Morrison was mysterious', said John later, 'I dug that.'

Ray and Jim, meanwhile, were knocked out by John's jazzy drumming. John Densmore was in the band.

It was only a fortnight later that the band went down to World Pacific recording studios on Third Street, Los Angeles. Rick and the Ravens were owed three hours recording time, and Ray wanted to get the new band down on acetate to hear what it sounded like. With only one or two takes, they recorded six tracks, all songs Jim had written in that summer burst, including 'Moonlight Drive', 'End of the Night' and 'Hello, I Love You'.

As Ray, Dorothy and Jim drove off afterwards in their yellow VW Beetle, Jim beamed in the back seat. It was the first time he had heard his voice. He liked it.

The record companies, however, did not: nor his songs, nor the band's sound. Day after day Jim, Ray, Dorothy and John trooped around record companies with the disc. They were rejected by everyone.

The band resumed rehearsals half-heartedly. And then Rick and Jim Manczarek quit. As regulars on the club gig circuit, they regarded Jim's singing as unprofessional. Ray and John said they thought they were making a mistake. The band was going to be big.

Besides, Jim's voice was developing a distinctive, soul-scraping 'brass and leather' sound. More than this, Jim was metamorphosing before their eyes into a rock and roll star. He had lost 30 pounds in weight and was now lean-hipped and sinewy. The puppy-fat on his face had melted away, revealing a face that was Ancient Greek beautiful, framed perfectly by his lion's mane hair. A veritable pop Adonis.

The 'Lizard King'

Jim was friends with Andy Warhol

To help fill the gap left by the departed Manczarek brothers, John suggested a friend from University High School who had since played with him in an occasional band called the Psychedelic Rangers. He was also in the same meditation class as John and Ray.

Robby Krieger, a frizzy-haired 19-year-old introvert, seemed unlikely material for a rock band. Ray worried about Robby's shyness at the audition but was 'blown away' by his playing of a bottle-neck on his electric guitar. (It was a technique Robby had picked up from old blues players, who slid the broken-off neck of a beer bottle along the fret to produce an eerie howl.) Ray also acknowledged that Robby's intricate flamenco and folk-style of playing might add something to the band's sound.

Krieger, Densmore, Ray Manczarek – or Manzarek, as he now called himself – and Morrison. The Doors line up was complete.

The band almost ended before it began. Out of the blue Jim, John and Robby were called up for the draft, next stop the Vietnam War. (Ray had already done some military service, getting an early discharge by pretending homosexuality.) Aside from their commitment to their music, none of the three identified with US policy in Vietam, or the idea of military discipline. To avoid the draft John claimed to be gay and Robby's rich parents hired a psychiatrist to say he was unfit for service.

Jim took a load of drugs, hyping up his heart-rate and blood pressure, told the draft board he was queer and that they would rue the day they put him in uniform. He was refused service.

And so the band rehearsed on, every day, getting tighter and closer, developing what they later called a 'oneness'.

Everything came together at a rehearsal early in the New Year 1966, at Robby's parents' place on Pacific Pallisades. The evening before Jim had suggested that everyone write a song that night using universal imagery. Jim's song was 'The End', a haunting lament to lost love, destined to gather more and more meaning as the years would roll on. It would be Jim's epitaph ('This is the end my only friend'), and the anthem of the US Army 'grunts' in the Ah Shau Valley as they faced the 'gooks' in the maelstrom of Vietnam.

Robby also had a song, which was worked on first, as it seemed easier to arrange. During a beer break, while Ray composed an intro, Jim said that he thought that they should divide evenly all the money the band made, including the songwriting money. Since Jim was the main songwriter it was a generous offer although, as he pointed out himself, all the band was sharing in the arranging.

The rehearsal resumed, the band feeling more than ever like a family, everyone trying out things to Robby's song. John struck a 3/4 jazz tempo on his brushes, Ray joined in with a carnival organ sound, and Jim started singing the first verse of Robby's 'Light My Fire'. Just as they were getting going, Jim looked up from Robby's notepaper. 'Hey, Robby, where's the rest of it?'

'I got stuck after the first verse', explained Robby.

At this Jim rolled his eyes, thought for a moment, and then invented the second verse as he stood there. Everyone came together in the chorus, blasting out the last lines: 'Try to set the night on – FI-YERRRRRRRR.'

That same week, after pestering every club-owner on Sunset Strip, they got their first proper gig, playing at the London Fog. The owner's terms were a miserly $5 a night, and most of the clientele were drunken sailors and perverts, but it gave them a chance to hone their act.

To the band's surprise Bill James, head of Artists and Repertoire for Columbia Records, dropped into the club to see them. He had heard their demo, liked it, and wanted to sign them up. They were ecstatic.

The joy was short-lived. After the signing, Columbia hardly contacted the band. When John went to the Columbia office to see what was going on, he noticed the Doors' name on the 'Drop List'.

They were then fired from the Fog.

However, their luck turned again almost immediately. On the very night they played their last gig at the London Fog, the talent-booker from the Whisky-A-Go-Go, Sunset Strip's trendiest club, signed them up.

The band played at the Whisky-A-Go-Go from mid-May to mid-July 1966, despite being fired almost every night by the club's owners for their stage antics. Jim, who was already consuming drugs in quantities that made the rest of the band – no strangers themselves to illicit substances – nervous, came in for special opprobrium. Some nights he was too blitzed to turn up. But they were hired again every morning because 'chicks' kept ringing in to find out when the horny guy in black pants was singing next, and the band was developing a following amongst the underground crowd for their music. The word on the street was 'See the Doors, they're the hottest band in town'.

And then the Whisky-A-Go-Go fired them – definitely, irrevocably – after an incident which has become part of rock mythology.

The club lights were down, and Jim started singing 'The End' as though it was a funeral oration. The swaying, stoned crowd fell silent, and even the go-go dancers in their cages stopped moving to watch. The musical accompaniment was as haunting as the singing, with heart-thumps from Ray's organ, weird, Eastern riffs from Robby's guitar, and spine-chilling bursts from John's drums.

Every time Jim performed 'The End' he liked to extemporise, add in chunks of poetry. This evening, he had an extra surprise in store. As he went into the last verse, he started an Oedipal rap about a killer waking before dawn, walking down the hall of his home, into his sister's room, his brother's room, then his parents' room – where he told his father that he wanted to kill him, and told his mother: 'I want to F—— YOU!'

The last line was delivered in a primal scream. There was no mistaking what was said.

When, after the performance, the Doors went into the artists' lounge, the Whiskey-A-Go-Go's co-owner, Phil Tanzini, told Jim he was a foul-mouthed sonofabitch and that the Doors were fired. To underline the point he had them ejected from the club.

Not that it mattered. The Doors had just been offered a recording deal by Jac Holzman, president of the small Elektra company, with an advance of $5,000. To celebrate, Ray, John and Robby bought new equipment. Jim bought a custom leather suit.

Jim's song 'The End' was used for the film *Apocalypse Now*

The 'superstar' on stage

The Doors were flown to New York for the official signing, and a month of Elektra-organized gigs at Ondine's disco. The gigs were a triumph, with pop artist Andy Warhol and his entourage regularly taking stage-side seats. Jim became an official 'superstar' (Warhol invented the phrase). One night Warhol gave Jim a gold French phone which Jim, drunk, threw in a rubbish bin.

It was in New York that the Mr Hyde in Jim's Dr Jekyll began to emerge more fully. The drug-assisted explorations of his own mind and the heavy recreational drinking had started to take their toll. The games Jim liked to play started to become dangerous, unpredictable. Once, when Paul Rothchild, the producer Elektra had assigned to the Doors, drove the band back to the Henry Hudson Hotel, Jim started ripping Paul's hair out, causing the car to swerve almost off the road. When they reached the hotel Jim stripped stark naked and stood screaming on the window ledge of his tenth-storey room. Eventually he was persuaded to come in.

In November the band returned to LA, where they started recording their first album at Sunset Sound Studios.

It was around this time that Jim moved in with Pamela Courson, a doe-like, red-haired 18-year-old who had lived in Laurel Canyon. Though Jim would have many other girlfriends and one-night stands in his time (and Pam would prove no monogamist herself), he would always return to her. She was, he once said, his 'cosmic mate'. Pam referred to herself as Jim's wife and became known as Pamela Courson Morrison, although they never married officially. She would be the inspiration for many of Jim's songs, 'Love Street', written by Jim on the balcony of their apartment, 'Road House Blues' and 'Queen of the Highway' among them. As would become obvious over the years, the songs for Pamela always contained a bitter twist, a refusal to commit emotionally or a sardonic reference to their rocky romance. 'I guess I like it fine . . . so far' goes the play-out line of 'Love Street'.

Pam, meanwhile, had a guilty secret she kept from Jim. She was a heroin user. Jim hated heroin. It was the one drug he would not touch.

The last days of 1966 were spent hanging out at Elektra's small LA office. To accompany the album, the four Doors each wrote a biographical sketch, with Jim's a crafted, evocative statement of where he, and the band, were at:

'On stage the Doors look like they're in their own world. The songs are space-like & ancient. It sounds like carnival music. When it ends, there is a second of silence. Something new has come into the room.

You could say it's an accident that I was ideally suited for the work I am doing;

At the Morrison Hotel

The compulsive dreamer

it's the feeling of a bow string being pulled back for 22 years and suddenly let go. I am primarily an American; second, a Californian; third, a Los Angeles resident. I've always been attracted to ideas that were about revolt against authority – when you make your peace with authority you become an authority. I like ideas about the breaking away or overthrowing of the established order – I am interested in anything about revolt, disorder, chaos, especially activity that seems to have no meaning.'

Entitled simply *TheDoors*, the album was released in the first week of January 1967, along with the single 'Break on Through'. Elektra organized a signboard on Sunset Strip with a picture of the band and the legend 'THE

DOORS – Break on Through with an Electrifying Album', the first time a billboard was used on the Strip to promote a band.

The momentum was building. On the Wednesday the Doors went to San Francisco to attend – along with 20,000 hippies – the 'Human Be-In' at Golden Gate, the counter-culture event of the year. That night the Doors played the city's Fillmore Auditorium, America's finest rock venue. They were third on the bill to the Young Rascals and Sopwith Camel but they hypnotized the audience, hundreds leaving to spread the word 'Doors' around the streets.

Meanwhile, the single rose to number 11 in the LA charts, even making the bottom of the nationals, helped a little by the Doors' friends, who kept ringing radio stations to request it.

For most of the spring of 1967 the band stayed in California, playing clubs and concert halls, and arranging an edited-down version of 'Light My Fire', judged too long at seven minutes for a 45. Uninterested in the technical aspects of record-making, Jim drank all day at the bars on the Strip, until he lapsed into unconsciousness or had to get up on stage. Alcohol was becoming Jim's drug of choice; the psychedelics were being dropped in favour of Chivas Regal, Courvoisier and whisky.

But by the summer, there was no doubt about the band's success. By the end of

July the Doors' 'Light My Fire' was number 1. It would remain there for a month.

They had made it to the top.

Strange Days

The Jim Morrison of 1967 looked like a rock 'n' roll deity, darkly beautiful, broodingly tragic, Adonis but also Dionysus. In black leather pants he stood at the mike, intense, hip-cocked, oozing danger and sex. The stage performances got more theatrical, more amazing. Trance-like, usually drunk, perhaps stoned, he was an electric shaman, suddenly coming alive to the music, doing his one-footed-around-the-camp-fire-

Indian-dance, maybe his high dive into the audience. He could really play the audience now, getting them into a state of anticipation, then into what he called 'a peaking experience'.

In August, with 'Light My Fire' still riding high in the charts, the band went back into the studio to record their second album. The advance orders for *Strange Days* numbered a record-breaking 500,000.

Although Jim's vocal performances were strong, his unpredictability in the recording studio caused everyone to be uneasy. 'You never knew', said Paul Rothchild years later, 'whether Jim would show up as the erudite poetic scholar or the kamikaze drunk.'

Jim and Pamela moved to Paris in 1971

Père Lachaise cemetery, home to the famous

His lyric brilliance was undimmed, however. There was the haunting personal acknowledgement of his own alienation in 'People Are Strange', and the aggressive preoccupation with his own death in 'When the Music's Over'. The same song was also a generational anthem ('We want the world/And we want it now!'). America was becoming divided into conservative and radical, old and young, with the dividing line being Vietnam, a war in which young people, as they saw it, were sent to die by the old. As Jim said at the time the Doors 'could not help but reflect what is going on around us'. He would write his most militant songs in this year, 1967, including the anti-war 'Unknown Soldier', which the band performed on stage in dramatic fashion, with Jim assuming the position of a victim before a firing squad, collapsing to a 'bang' from John's drums.

Jim was not, ultimately, a political writer. He was only a rider on the storm of 1960s radical protest; apart from a dislike of authority and conformity, the truths he sought were universal, and he believed that the way to them was paved with sex, drugs, rock 'n' roll, and shamanism. Although the Doors evolved out of the 'All You Need Is Love' ethos of the beautiful generation, there was always a darkness about them. They were the shadow side of flower power.

The days of 1967, meanwhile, got stranger. Hitting the big time meant the Doors were criss-crossing the United States, east to west, north to south. As well as drinking, Jim was getting through a steady stream of groupies, one-night stands and girlfriends, although Pamela remained his number one. In New York Jim was introduced to the famous German vamp Nico, then singing with the Velvet Underground. Their relationship continued off and on for some time. 'Jim iss totally crazy', she told the press, admiration in her voice.

The Doors were now getting big media attention, and not just from teen magazines. No other band, before or since, has had such a spectrum of fandom, from young girls who sighed Jim's name into their pillows to serious, egghead rock critics, like Richard Goldstein at *Village*

Voice who said, perceptively, that Jim's lyrics were 'rock literature'. Another *Village Voice* writer claimed that Jim was the new male sex symbol, now that James Dean was dead and Marlon Brando had a paunch.

The increasingly wild side of Jim Morrison was displayed at a concert at New Haven, Connecticut, on 5 December 1967. Just before the band were due to go on stage, a policeman caught Jim necking with a fan in a shower room. The cop, not realizing who Jim was, instructed him to leave: 'Nobody allowed back here!' Jim told him to get lost. The argument escalated – and the cop sprayed mace in Jim's face. Jim hollered and the Doors crew came and rescued him, his eyes were washed and the matter seemed sorted. The show went on.

Then, half way through 'Back Door Man', Jim started a rap about what had happened backstage. The audience sat fascinated. Jim taunted the police standing at the front of the auditorium, there supposedly to protect the band from over enthusiastic fans. The police turned around, angry. Then the house lights went up and a police lieutenant arrived on stage and told Jim he was under arrest. Jim thrust the microphone under his face: 'Say your thing, man!' More cops appeared, dragged Jim away, kicked him and took him to the police station where he was charged with a breach of the peace. Jim Morrison had just become the first rock singer to be arrested on stage.

With hindsight, the other Doors would say that New Haven was the beginning of the end, the moment when things started to get out of control.

Jim Morrison's grave

The Doors after Jim Morrison

Someone Not Quite At Home

A roll of fat appeared around Jim's waist. He shaved less, and let his luxuriant hair go greasy. He moved into room 32 of the downtown $10-a-night Alta Cienega Motel, 100 yards from the Doors' offices – and just a short walk from his favourite bars on Sunset Strip.

By 1968 Jim was losing interest in being a rock star. The recording of the third album, *Waiting for the Sun*, had taken forever, partly because Paul Rothchild wanted a technically perfect record, partly because Jim used the studio as a place to party with his buddies, among them the Warhol actor Tom Baker and aspiring singer Alice Cooper.

One night John Densmore had had enough of Jim's drunkenness and quit. He came back the next day, but the Doors started hiring minders for Jim, someone who could keep a watch on his drinking, or at least get him to the gig or studio on time.

Everybody who met Jim came away with a different impression of him. Drunk. Southern Gentleman (always stood up when a woman entered a room, always tried to be polite in conversation, once gave the coat off his back to a shivering fan). Soft spoken Poet. Lothario. Madman. Artist with integrity (he was deeply dismayed when Buick used 'Light My Fire' for a commercial). Male Barbie Doll. Genius. In truth he was all of these, and more. One of his most enduring characteristics was loyalty to the other Doors. When the band's managers suggested to him that he go solo, he told the other Doors and suggested they dump their management.

The English leg of the band's 1968 European tour was filmed as a documentary, 'The Doors Are Open', by a TV company, to which Jim gave one of his most poignant quotes. He said of the Doors' music: 'The mood I get from most of it is a heavy, kind of a gloomy feeling – like of someone not quite at home, you know, not quite relaxed, aware of quite a lot of things, but not quite sure of anything . . . I'd like to do a song of pure joy, a pure expression of joy.' Jimmy Morrison, the military kid, dragged from base to base, never was at home.

By 1969 the Doors were the biggest group in America, and the pressures of stardom were becoming harder to bear. The audiences at the concerts expected more and more of outrageous Jim Morrison, self-styled 'Lizard King'. Somehow he had to entertain them beyond their expectations, go further and further out on the edge. And he drank to a degree that amazed even the seen-everything bartenders on Sunset Strip.

Robbie Krieger with the album *LA Woman*

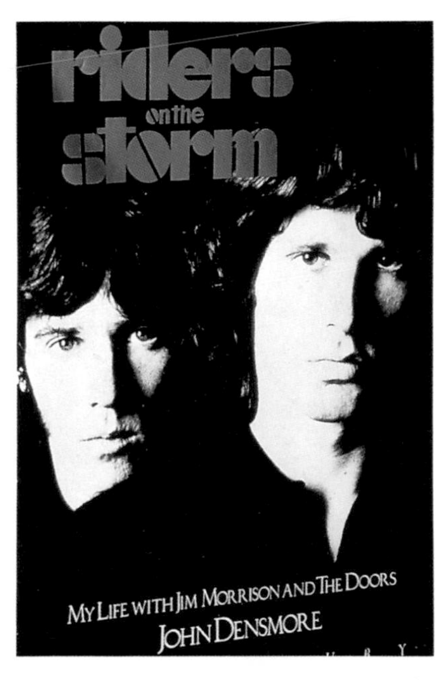

John Densmore's account of his life with the Doors

And so Jim arrived in Miami on 3 March, 1969, the day the Doors finally fell from grace. The night was hot, and the Dinner Key Auditorium was sweltering with the extra thousand people the promoter had crammed in. Jim had missed the arranged flight down, and arrived almost too drunk to stand. The band went on late, at 11 p.m., the crowd chanting 'Morrison, Morrison, Morrison'.

Just a few lines into 'Back Door Man' Jim, now sporting a dark beard, stopped singing and went into a drunken rap, insulting the audience, telling them they were idiots. He had already managed to make audiences riot in the past; tonight he had something else in mind.

Suddenly he shouted 'Let's get naked', and threw his shirt into the crowd. 'You didn't come here for music', he continued. 'You came for something else. Something greater than you've ever seen.'

A roar came up from the crowd, as Jim intimated he was going to strip his pants off, strip all the way.

Ray yelled at Vince Treanor, the Doors' electrician, to stop Jim, and Vince, bounding across the stage, managed to get his fingers in Jim's belt loops, stopping him.

The stadium went into uproar. A security man accidentally flipped Jim into the audience, where Jim started leading a snake dance followed by ten thousand people.

After a few days' holiday in Jamaica Jim flew back to the States to find that a warrant had been issued for his arrest for offences allegedly committed at the Miami concert. Jim was charged with indecent exposure, public profanity, drunkenness and – a felony – lewd and lascivious beviour ('did expose his penis'). If convicted Jim faced a possible sentence of seven and a half years at Raiford penitentiary. It made headline news coast to coast.

The effect was dramatic. Every city in the Doors' upcoming tour cancelled. The band was banned.

At the end of March the FBI charged Jim with unlawful flight, claiming that he left Miami to avoid prosecution. This was nonsense – Jim left for his well publicized holiday *before* any charges were filed – but none the less serious. The 'Lizard King' surrendered to the FBI on 4 April, and was released on $5,000 bail.

The trial was set for a year hence, April 1970. In the meantime, the anti-Doors hysteria continued. Few US venues would host them, even with a $5,000 bond posted against obscenity. At the shows which did happen, police stood waiting in the wings with blank arrest warrants.

It was necessary that the band find concert work. The new album, *Soft-Parade*, had cost $86,000. One solution was playing outside the USA, and a series of concerts at a Mexico City nightclub proved amongst the best in recent memory. Jim was impressed to find that his Oedipal 'The End' had been a hit single south of the border.

The advantage of the concert famine for Jim was that it gave him more time for his poetry and film interests. With the help of poet friend Michael McClure, Jim had two volumes of writing printed privately in 1969. *The New Creatures* was a collection of poetry exploring, often in nightmarish images, his personal anguish. The other book, *The Lords*, was a series of observations on cinematography. On both, the title page read: James Douglas Morrison. Within a year the two books would be published as a single volume by a major publishing house, Simon & Schuster. Encouraged, Jim wrote a long poem, 'American Prayer', a state of the union address, which appeared in *Rolling Stone* magazine.

The outcome of Jim's film projects, though, was disappointing. A documentary about the Doors entitled *Feast of Friends*, made with Jim's and Ray's friends from UCLA, and a film about hitch-hiking, *HWY*, were almost universally received as amateurish, incomplete. Reluctantly Jim came to accept that it would be as a rock singer and lyricist – a rock 'n' roll poet – that he would truly make his mark. The Doors' next album, *Morrison Hotel*, named after a real downtown LA hotel, was a lyrical masterpiece, Jim's strongest work in years. Even the doubters were forced to acknowledge that the Doors, and Jim especially, could still turn it on.

Paris

On Monday 10 August 1970 Jim Morrison entered the Metropolitan Dade County Justice Building, the defendant in case 69-2355. Jim's lawyer, Max Fink, had nearly 100 witnesses lined up to testify that Jim did not expose himself. Max also had a powerful argument that the charges against Jim were unconstitutional, undermining theatrical freedom, and that nothing Jim had said or done on stage was out of the ordinary compared with contemporary social and artistic standards. Much 'dirtier' material could be heard any night of the week from stand-up comics at Miami hotels.

No sooner had the trial begun than Patricia Kennely arrived in Miami: she was pregnant with Jim's child. Jim had been seeing the 24-year-old editor of *Jazz & Pop* magazine for almost a year, and had even gone to the altar with her on Midsummer's night in a witches wedding. They had signed their names in blood and Jim – phobic about sharp instruments – had fainted.

Jim persuaded Kennely to have an abortion, telling her that he could not be responsible for a child.

The Miami trial staggered on for over a month, with Judge Murray Goodman allowing recesses for the Doors to play some previously arranged concerts, including one on the Isle of Wight in England. Almost in the same breath he refused any evidence about artistic standards, ruling out at a stroke a main plank of Jim's defence. Most court days were taken up with witness testimonies. A moment of light relief came when Ray Manzarek was asked if he had seen Mr Morrison's organ on stage in Miami. 'No I didn't, your honour', replied Ray, 'but I play organ.' (Ray would say later that he thought a 'mass hallucination' had taken place at Miami; Jim did not expose himself, and had even been wearing underwear that night, something he rarely did.)

Jim Morrison was found guilty of public exposure and profanity – both misdemeanours – but innocent of the other charges. At a deferred session in October Judge Goodman sentenced Jim to eight months' hard labour at Dade County Jail. He was also fined $500. Jim remained free on $50,000 bail pending an appeal.

Things got worse. Jimi Hendrix died, followed in quick succession by Janis Joplin. 'I'm gonna be number three', Jim started telling friends.

Pamela left him for a French count.

Yet despite the personal traumas, Jim was writing well, producing material for the Doors' new album, *LA Woman*, including

'Riders on the Storm' and the title track, a bleak commentary on Los Angeles. ('LA Woman' contained a celebrated anagram of Jim Morrison, 'Mr Mojo Risin'', 'mojo' being black slang for sexual prowess.) After an argument with their perfectionist producer, Paul Rothchild, who complained about tensions in the band and the 'boring' nature of the songs, the Doors produced the record themselves with engineer Bruce Botnick. With the recording done at the Doors' rehearsal room – in which Jim's vocal booth was a bathroom – the result, exactly suiting the lyrics, had a raw, bluesy feel. It was almost like starting over.

On Jim's 27th birthday, 8 December 1970, as a present to himself, he recorded some of his poetry. He liked the result, and the high lasted for days. A Doors concert in Dallas on 11 December was a delerious success.

And then the music was over. On the following night in New Orleans Jim crumpled. Those who were there said you could see his will and energy leave him.

Jim Morrison never performed with the Doors again.

A bright spot was that Pamela returned to Los Angeles, and Jim moved back in with her. Something approaching domestic bliss ensued, even when Jim spent Christmas night huddled under a quilt with the visiting Patricia Kennely.

Early in New Year 1971, Jim thought he'd like to get away from Los Angeles, America, his life. Paris was an obvious choice, he had been there several times and liked it. And it was the traditional place for artistic Americans to go abroad, ever since the time of Gertrude Stein and Ernest Hemingway.

Pam loved the idea. They left their labrador dog, Sage, with Pam's parents, and Pam flew on ahead to find an apartment. Jim spent a few days clearing out his desk at the Doors' office, saying goodbye to friends, and to several of his more regular girlfriends.

He left for Paris on 16 March.

The End

For a while Paris was good. Jim and Pam got on well, and the city sights were a distraction from the pressures of being Jim Morrison. He walked the city ceaselesly, an anonymous figure. Old friends dropped by, new ones were made. A trip to Spain, Morocco and Corsica, playing tourist, was idyllic. He even cut down on his drinking, shaved, and was persuaded by Pam to wear something other than his battle jacket.

At the end of June Jim phoned John Densmore back in LA to find out how *LA Woman* just released, was doing. He placed another call to Bill Siddons, the Doors' manager, and told him he was working on some great new songs.

But almost immediately Jim went into a pit of depression. The demons were back. The work wasn't going well. He sat motionless at the dining-room table in their Left Bank apartment for hours, nothing coming from his pen. Pam and his friends tried to shake him out of it, but he had withdrawn deep inside.

The rumours that Jim was dead hit Los Angeles on the morning of Monday 5 July. Bill Siddons phoned Pamela in

Paris; she told him to come over right away. Siddons arrived in Paris on Tuesday morning and was greeted at the Morrisons' flat by Pamela and a sealed coffin. She had a death certificate in her hand, signed by a French doctor.

The next day, with Pam, Bill and three friends in attendance, the Lizard King was buried at Père La Chaise cemetery, the home in death to some of Jim's literary heros, such as Balzac and Oscar Wilde.

Over twenty years on, and the mystery of Jim's death still lingers on. Did he die or was the death an elaborate trick so that he could assume another, easier, life? And if Jim died, how did he die?

The evidence is contradictory. There are regular sightings of Jim Morrison – as there are of Elvis – but almost certainly Jim met his end in Paris that weekend. Some say Jim went to a rock club on the evening of Friday 2 July, and took an overdose of some unidentified drug, dying in the lavatory. The 'official' version, as given to the press by Bill Siddons, is that Jim died of a heart attack in the early hours of Saturday 3 July, in the bath, where he was discovered by Pamela, who tried to revive him.

What Exactly happened on the night of Jim's death may never be known. The one person who could say never did, and took her secret to the grave. Pamela died of an overdose in 1974.

She did let slip some details, though, and some of her friends have talked off the record. It seems that Jim died of a heroin overdose, possibly suicidal, possibly accidental. Though Jim hated heroin he would try anything once – more than once – and may have been past caring anyway. Pam herself was a regular heroin user, and there was a stash of the drug at the Paris apartment. According to this version, Jim took the drug and went into the bathroom – when Pamela could get no reply, she called over her sometime French lover, Count Jean DeBretti, and Marianne Faithfull. They kicked down the bathroom door – and there was Jim lying dead in the bathtub.

Jim Morrison had finally broken on through to the other side.